Apple

Apple

Vern Thiessen

Playwrights Canada Press
Toronto • Canada

Apple © Copyright 2002 Vern Thiessen
The author asserts moral rights.

Playwrights Canada Press
54 Wolseley St., 2nd fl. Toronto, Ontario CANADA M5T 1A5
416-703-0013   fax 416-703-0059
orders@playwrightscanada.com • www.playwrightscanada.com

CAUTION: This play is fully protected under the copyright laws of Canada and all other countries of The Copyright Union, and is subject to royalty. Changes to the script are expressly forbidden without the prior written permission of the author. Rights to produce, film, or record, in whole or in part, in any medium or any language, by any group, amateur or professional, are retained by the author. For amateur or professional production rights, please contact:
Charles Northcote, The Core Group, 507 – 3 Church Street, Toronto, Ontario M5E 1M2 416-955-0819   literary@coregroupta.com

No part of this book, covered by the copyright hereon, may be reproduced or used in any form or by any means—graphic, electronic or mechanical—without the prior written permission of the publisher except for excerpts in a review. Any request for photocopying, recording, taping or information storage and retrieval systems of any part of this book shall be directed in writing to The Canadian Copyright Licensing Agency, 1 Yonge St., Suite 1900, Toronto, Ontario CANADA M5E 1E5 416-868-1620.

Playwrights Canada Press acknowledges the support of the taxpayers of Canada and the province of Ontario through The Canada Council for the Arts and the Ontario Arts Council.

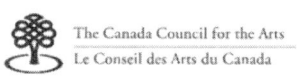 

Cover photo of Coralie Cairns (front) and Shaun Johnston (shadow) by Russ Hewitt.
Production Editor: Jodi Armstrong

National Library of Canada Cataloguing in Publication Data

Thiessen, Vern
　Apple

A play.
ISBN 0-88754-638-2

I. Title.

PS8589.H4524S76 2002   C812'.54   C2002-900092-0
PR9199.3.T4486A66 2002

First edition: June 2002.
Printed and bound by AGMV Marquis at Quebec, Canada.

to Eden, for healing me

and

for Sandra, who I never met

ACKNOWLEDGMENTS

I would like to thank the following organizations which have assisted in the development of this play: the Edmonton Community Lottery Board, the Alberta Foundation for the Arts, the Banff/ATP PlayRites Colony (1999), Workshop West's Springboards New Play Festival (2000), the New Play Festival at Playwrights Theatre Centre (2001) in Vancouver, the Alberta Playwriting Competition, Original Sin Productions, the Unconscious Collective, Alberta Playwrights Network, the board, staff and volunteers of Workshop West Theatre, and The Blue Heron Theatre in New York City.

I would also like to thank the following individuals for their assistance and commitment: Eden Philp, Trevor Schmidt, David Mann, Rachel Ditor, Chapelle Jaffe, Shona Neil, Doug Barron, Ardelle Striker, Leslie (Hoban) Blake, Greg Nelson, Aaron Bushkowsky, Katrina Dunn, Kathryn Bracht, Cavin Cunnigham, Trenna Keating, Bill Hales, Pheobe Jonas, Margaret Reed, Hamilton Clancy, Charles Northcote, Randy White, Michael Nathanson, Andy Houston, and all the actors, stage managers and designers involved with workshopping the play. A special thanks to Ron Jenkins, whose uncompromising passion and vision is truly inspiring.

Apple was commissioned by Workshop West Theatre, Edmonton in 1999. It was first produced by Workshop West on April 11, 2002 at the Kaasa Theatre, Edmonton with the following cast:

ANDY   Shaun Johnston
EVELYN   Coralie Cairns
SAMANTHA Daniela Vlaskalic

Directed by Ron Jenkins
Stage Managed by Cheryl Millikin
Set, Props, Costumes and Lighting Design by Narda McCarroll
Original Music and Sound Design by Dave Clarke
Production Manager: Scott Peters
Production Assistant: Tandi McLeod
Carpenters: Bobby Smale and Scott Peters
General Manager: Shona Neil

A shorter version of *Apple* was first produced by The Unconscious Collective at the 1998 Edmonton Fringe Festival.

CHARACTERS

ANDY   a man
EVELYN   his wife
SAMANTHA   a medical student

SETTING

A park overlooking a lake.

TIME

The present.

PRODUCTION NOTE

The play should flow from scene to scene, but not quickly. Scene breaks are only indicated for rehearsal purposes. Much of the play's action lies in the "unspoken." Although not all pauses are created equally, the term *pause* is an important aspect of the play's action and rhythm. Theatricality and non-naturalism in design is encouraged. Both Act One and Act Two should run *no less* than 40 minutes each. In the original production, the intermission and the first scene of Act Two were removed, in favour of the following movement/music sequence:

> *LYN stares across the lake. She begins to pare down, SAM and ANDY assisting her: skirt and blouse removed, replaced by a hospital gown; hair put up, replaced by a handkerchief; makeup wiped away, replaced with nothing but her skin.*

Potential producers are free to use either choice. As this text went to print shortly after the play's premiere, please consult the playwright's agent for any further updates to the text before production.

ACT ONE

> *ANDY overlooking the lake. SAM watches him. LYN in a different world.*

ANDY *(to audience)* I bite into her breast.

LYN *(smiles)* Careful...

ANDY She says. I bite into her breast. Testing her flesh. Teasing her skin, tasting her fruit. Until her mind shudders...

LYN Careful...

ANDY *(smiles)* She says.

LYN They're not apples.

≈ ≈ ≈

SAM Good morning. *(unsure)* As you can see, this seminar will examine "Dysfunction in Cell Differentiation and Proliferation." We tend to treat this as a... simple concept. But in fact, it is represented by a highly complex sequence of events....

≈ ≈ ≈

LYN Hi.

ANDY Hey.

LYN *(surprised)* You're home.

ANDY Yeah.

LYN Christ what a day.

ANDY Oh?

LYN Goddamn bitch.

ANDY Who.

LYN Darlene.

ANDY Ah.

LYN Get groceries?

ANDY No.

LYN Shit. Trying to tell me how to do my job. There is nothing to eat in this house.

ANDY Lyn, I...

LYN Did you pick up the stuff?

ANDY The...?

LYN The dry cleaning?

ANDY Oh. No.

LYN Andy! I have a meeting first thing, I need that dry cleaning, I *need* it. I'm hungry, there's no food in the house, I've got a headache, did you pick up the Adv–?

ANDY No.

LYN Christ, I'm going to kill you. It's bad enough I have to deal with that bitch without–

ANDY Sorry, but–

LYN I said "go fuck yourself" is what I said "Darlene." I mean I didn't say that but I did.

She relishes it.

"I don't give a shit" I said "who your clients are, I have till tomorrow nine PM to close the deal, and that's how long we're going to take. I don't care princess" I said "who they are, or what they wear, or what constituency they represent, or what they look like, or who they play golf with or who they fuck. I don't care." I have a responsibility to my client, the balls in my court, I'm going to play it. "So don't try to rush me or push me or pull any of that political bullshit–" *(to ANDY)* You didn't wear that today did you?

She presses on.

So what happens? She goes off on some *thing*, some tangent, telling me I don't know what I'm doing. Me. *I* don't know what I'm doing! "These people" she says "they're this, they're that, they're blah blah blah, you can't *do* this to people like this." Well guess what. I've been in this business fifteen years and fuck if I'm going to be pushed around by some airhead thinks she knows something. She knows shit, and she knows she knows shit, and so I say "Darlene: you know shit. That's why I'm number one in the city, and you honey, are a fucking bottom dweller. You want some advice?" I say, "do some sit-ups, for Christ sakes, get a fucking makeover." And know what she does then? Know what she does?

ANDY Lyn, I–

LYN She throws coffee at me.

She *throws* her *coffee* at me. Hot, scalding – a moccachino yet – all over my skirt – which is why I *really need* that dry–. So what do I do? I run to the parking lot. Little does Ms Fuck Head know, but I carry an extra skirt in the back of the car. Fifteen years, I'm prepared for anything. So. I'm in the back seat, pulling off the moccachino skirt—not going to change in the office, not going to give her the pleasure—when I see it. I gotta run in my hose. I gotta run looks like a, a, a varicose vein leaking down my brand new hose. So there I am: no skirt, bare legs, it's like five degrees, my naked ass is freezing to the backseat, when I remember. I remember I always carry an extra pair in my briefcase. Fifteen years, I'm prepared for anything. I bolt into action: Pull off the old skirt, pull off the old hose, pull on the new hose, pull on the new skirt, wipe the coffee from my blouse—don't have an extra blouse, but luckily I'm wearing the navy blazer—check the mirror: lipstick, powder, a quick brush of the hair, and I'm as good as new. In fact, I'm *better* than new. Run across the parking lot, stroll in the door, see Darlene, walk up to her, and look her in the eye. And you know what I do? Know what I do?

Pause.

(triumphant) I. Do. Nothing.

She is beneath me. She is a floor below. Consummate professional I am. Proceed as if nothing happened. And do you *think* she says anything? Do you think she says a thing to me? Does she?

ANDY I've been fired.

Pause.

Twenty minutes to clear off my desk. Twenty minutes for ten years. Ten years.

Pause.

LYN Great. That's just great.

≈ ≈ ≈

SAM As we, as we see here, cells from a primary neoplasm become autonomous, undergoing a physical separation from the primary tumour, and invading other cells. It's... it's as if the fidelity of the basement membrane is being challenged. You see?

≈ ≈ ≈

ANDY overlooking the lake. SAM watches him. She approaches.

SAM Beautiful day.

Pause.

ANDY Yes.

SAM   The lake.
ANDY Yes.
SAM   The trees.
ANDY Yes.
SAM   The park.
ANDY Mm.

    Pause.

SAM   I like it here.
ANDY Yeah.

    Pause.

SAM   Every day.
ANDY Hm?
SAM   Every day I see you. Here. Sitting. Every day.
ANDY Yeah.
SAM   Time off work?
ANDY Yeah. Uh, no. Not really, I...

    Pause.

Fired, downsized, whatever. Twenty minutes to clear off my desk. Twenty minutes for ten years. Ten years....

    Pause.

SAM   Now you can enjoy it.
ANDY Being laid off?
SAM   No silly. The park.

ANDY   Ah. Right. The park.

He smiles. She smiles.

SAM   Do you mind if I...?

ANDY   Of course not, I should have...

SAM   I hope I'm...

ANDY   No.

SAM   'Cause I don't want...

ANDY   Not at all.

SAM   I wouldn't want, you know, if you're...

ANDY   Please.

She sits. Pause.

You see. The problem is – with what you just said – the problem is: I loved my job.

SAM   Really? Loved?

ANDY   Yeah.

SAM   And what did you love?

ANDY   What did I...?

SAM   About your job.

ANDY   Well...

Pause.

What I did.

SAM   Ah.

ANDY   What I was doing.

SAM Uh huh.

ANDY It was... fun. It was... challenging. It was.... You know. The Government.

She laughs. He smiles.

You?

SAM I've never loved a job.

ANDY No no, I meant...

SAM Oh. I'm a, I'm a student. At the University.

ANDY Ah. And you don't love that? What you're studying?

SAM *(playful)* It's... fun, it's... challenging, it's... you know. The University.

They laugh. Pause.

No, never loved anything.

She looks out.

Except this day. I love this day.

ANDY Never really thought about it. The "day." Always inside.

SAM You see? What you've been missing?

ANDY I suppose.

She closes her eyes, suns her face. He watches.

ANDY So you come here...?

SAM *(eyes closed)* Every day. Almost. Don't live far from here. I have a beautiful view of this park. Beautiful....

She suns herself. He watches.

ANDY   And you, what, you come here and you…

SAM   I just… listen.

ANDY   Ah.

SAM   To the day. The time. The moment.

ANDY   The…?

SAM   The moment.

ANDY   I'm not sure….

SAM   Try it.

ANDY   What, you mean…?

SAM   Close your eyes.

ANDY   Close my…?

SAM   For a second.

ANDY   I don't know, I…

SAM   Go on. Trust me.

Pause.

ANDY   Alright.

He closes his eyes.

SAM   Now just… listen.

ANDY   Okay.

SAM   *(slowly)* Imagine this day. See it in your mind. The sun on your face. The spring in your mouth. Your heart deep inside. No future. No past. No time. Just this day. This moment.

She moves closer.

This is the moment. When everything changes. When the sun sets. When the leaves fall. When the ice melts. When the air smells like sweet spring, or dying fall, or clean winter. When things change. Right now.

She is very close.

Open your eyes.

He does.

Well?

ANDY   …wow.

SAM   Did that… scare you?

ANDY   I….

SAM   Excite you?

ANDY   That depends on….

SAM   Turn you on?

ANDY   Uh, yeah, I uh, yeah, sure. *(recovering)* You see, I loved my job–

SAM   Shhh.

Her finger to his lips.

Listen.

ANDY   I…

SAM   Listen.

ANDY   I'm not sure…

SAM   Look at me.

He looks at her.

ANDY I don't....

SAM Shhh.

> *She places his hand on her breast.*

Do you hear it?

ANDY Yes.

SAM Do you?

ANDY Yes.

SAM Do you?

> *Pause.*

ANDY Yes.

> *He kisses her. She responds.*

≈ ≈ ≈

SAM (*undressing*) Shhh.

ANDY She says, and the sound leaps from her tongue.

SAM Shhh.

ANDY She says. Music rises from the well of her throat, and I drink.

SAM (*teasing*) Be patient.

ANDY She says. And I, who am older; I, who am to be softer; I, who am to be wiser; I, who am to know all these things....

SAM (*giggles*) Be patient.

ANDY ...know nothing. And learn from her, to...

SAM Be patient.

l to r:
Daniela Vlaskalic, Shaun Johnston.
Photographer: Russ Hewitt

ANDY   To…

SAM   Shhh.

ANDY   To…

SAM   Listen.

≈ ≈ ≈

LYN   Hi.

ANDY   Hey.

LYN   You're home.

ANDY   Yeah.

LYN   Christ what a day.

ANDY   Oh?

LYN   Goddamn bitch.

ANDY   Who.

LYN   Darlene.

ANDY   Ah.

LYN   Clean the bathroom?

ANDY   Nope.

LYN   Take out the garbage?

ANDY   No.

LYN   *Lift a fucking finger?*

Pause.

I know Andy.

ANDY	*(nervous)* What?
LYN	I know.
ANDY	Know what.
LYN	I know what you're going to say. "It's hard." Right?
ANDY	*(relieved)* Ah. Well…
LYN	It's hard when you don't have work. It's hard watching the walls, it's hard watching the dishes get dirty, it's hard watching the vacuum when it's turned on, it's hard watching the bills arrive, praying they'll pay themselves. It's so fucking hard. Maybe it's too much to ask. Maybe it's too much for you to either work at home, or get off your ass and–
ANDY	I had an interview today.

Pause.

As a matter of fact.

Pause.

LYN	Oh.
ANDY	Yeah.
LYN	And?
ANDY	Contract position. No pension, no medical.
LYN	And?
ANDY	A fraction of what I used to earn.
LYN	And?
ANDY	You really want to know?
LYN	Of course.

ANDY Because it might be *hard*, it might be *difficult*–

LYN Tell me!

ANDY Alright. Alright.

Pause.

So I walk into the room, and there's these three… kids, how they got where they are I have no idea. Half my age, twice the attitude, three times the confidence.

LYN Right.

ANDY One's in *jeans* if you can believe it, the other two have *nose rings*, that's new to me, and they're like, you know, off some TV show, that one, you know, the one where, what's it called…?

LYN Yeah yeah yeah.

ANDY And so they sit me down, and get me a, a, you know, one of those coffees you always order.

LYN A latte?

ANDY Yeah. And they start on the basic questions: who are you, tell us about yourself, why'd you leave your last position, you know.

LYN Uh huh.

ANDY And I'm feeling pretty good, I'm calm, I'm answering the questions, I feel like we're, you know, connecting on some level, like I might make it through this, like I might get this thing, like I can handle it, you know?

LYN Sure.

ANDY But then. Then it gets *really* – then they start in with the *real* questions.

LYN Like?

ANDY	They ask me about my skills in writing hyper text markup language. They ask about my ability to maintain their URL. They ask me if I'd feel comfortable heading up their e-commerce department. They ask me what considerations I'd take into account when setting up a cyber conference with seven stakeholders in seven different cities.
LYN	And?
ANDY	And?
LYN	What'd you say?
ANDY	What'd I–? I didn't know what the fuck they were *talking* about!
	Pause.
LYN	So?
ANDY	They might need someone in accounting. *Accounting.* Christ.
LYN	And?
ANDY	That was it. Showed me the door, nice meeting you, thanks for coming in, we'll get back to you.
LYN	"Get back to you?"
ANDY	Friday.
LYN	"Get back to you?"
ANDY	That's what they said.
LYN	"By Friday."
ANDY	Will you stop.
LYN	What.
ANDY	Stop it.

LYN	What!
ANDY	You're not being supportive.
LYN	You call that an interview?
ANDY	And what would *you* call it.
LYN	A blow-off, honey, that is what I call a fucking blow-off.
ANDY	Thanks, thanks a lot.
LYN	You have to be aggressive.
ANDY	Aggressive.
LYN	You've been in government too long.
ANDY	Have I.
LYN	You've got to learn to play the game.
ANDY	I know how to play the game.
LYN	Not out there you don't.
ANDY	I know.
LYN	Not out there.
ANDY	I KNOW.

Pause.

What do you want me to do? Huh? *Force* them to hire me? I'm trying. I'm at the paper . I'm at the employment office every day. I'm at the computer every day, surfing the goddamn e-mail.

LYN	Internet.
ANDY	You know what I mean. I'm trying. And you know what? It *is* hard. And I don't need you rubbing – I don't need you – I don't need you telling me–

LYN	I never said–
ANDY	It's not what you say Lyn, it's the way you look.
LYN	The way I what?
ANDY	That look.
LYN	What–
ANDY	There.
LYN	Give me a fucking–
ANDY	That look.
LYN	This is ridic–
ANDY	There again.
LYN	Andy.
ANDY	And again. That look. You look at me like I'm worthless. Like I'm stupid.
LYN	Stop it!
ANDY	*No you*! *You* stop it! You stop it with your "you're so stupid, why the fuck did I marry you" look. You stop it.

Pause.

That's what you're thinking. Isn't it? When you give me that look. Isn't it?

LYN	Andy.
ANDY	"…lousy husband, lousy lay…"
LYN	I never–
ANDY	Ah! But the look.

Pause.

> Uh?
>
> *Pause.*
>
> You know it's true. You know it.
>
> *Pause. She opens her arms.*

LYN Come here.

ANDY Why.

LYN I want to give you a hug.

ANDY No.

LYN Come here.

ANDY No. You come over *here* and give me a hug if you want to give me a hug.

> *She relents, comes to him. Hugs him.*

LYN Mmmmm.

ANDY Mmmmm.

> *He responds, nibbles her neck, begins undressing her, making his way to her breast.*

LYN ...Andy....

ANDY Remember the time.

LYN What....

ANDY That time in the house.

LYN What house.

ANDY The show home.

LYN Oh God.

ANDY	That big empty room.
LYN	That was years....
ANDY	The cool carpet.
LYN	My first sale.
ANDY	The fresh paint.
LYN	My first commission.
	He begins to make love to her.
ANDY	(*slowly*) And I laid you back. Back. Till we fell to the floor. The silence of new suburbs. And the windows, undressed. And the lights in the house. All of them. On. Burning. And we–
LYN	(*sharp pain*) AH!
ANDY	What.
LYN	Careful.
ANDY	What. What did I...?
LYN	They're not apples you know.
ANDY	I know!
	Pause.
	I know.
	Pause.
	Lyn. When are we–?
LYN	It's always the same.
ANDY	What?
LYN	It's predictable.

ANDY Is it.

LYN You think you know what I want.

ANDY That's because we never do it. If we did it–

LYN You never know what I want.

ANDY *You* don't know what you want, how am *I* supposed to–

LYN Fuck you.

ANDY No, fuck you.

LYN That's not true.

ANDY It is. You can't make up your mind.

LYN Maybe I *have* made up my mind.

ANDY Oh, oh really.

LYN Yeah.

ANDY 'Cause I'm just being "aggressive."

LYN Maybe it's not you.

Pause.

ANDY Now what's that supposed to mean.

Pause.

LYN Maybe I'm not sure anymore.

ANDY What if I said that to you.

LYN Maybe it's not right.

ANDY What if I said "maybe it's not you, Lyn."

LYN Maybe we need something different.

ANDY What if I said "I'm sleeping with someone else."

Pause.

LYN Excuse me? I never said that.

ANDY You, you know what I–

LYN I never said that.

Pause.

What's going on.

Pause.

Andy.

ANDY Nothing.

LYN Are you…?

ANDY What.

LYN Are you…?

ANDY *What*!

Pause.

LYN (*incredulous*) Are you screwing someone?

Pause.

ANDY What, you think I'm not capable of–

LYN I didn't say–

ANDY Because if that's what you–

LYN What the hell is–?

ANDY I just want things to be the way they were before.

LYN They can't.

ANDY I want to make things better.

LYN You can't.

ANDY I want things to be *different* then. I don't care. I just don't want this.

Pause.

LYN It's sick Andy. This marriage is ill.

ANDY Then let's see someone.

LYN We've been there.

ANDY Someone new. I hear there's a good therapist–

LYN It won't help.

ANDY What if – if we had a baby.

LYN Andy.

ANDY So what then.

LYN I don't know.

ANDY What can I do, tell me.

LYN I said I don't–

ANDY WHAT.

LYN *(fierce)* Nothing!

Pause.

Take out the garbage.

Pause.

And find a fucking job.

≈ ≈ ≈

ANDY I bite into her breast. Hard.

SAM That's it.

ANDY She says. I bite into her breast.

SAM I like it like that.

ANDY I bite, testing her flesh, teasing her skin, tasting her fruit, until her mind shudders–

SAM That's it.

ANDY She says.

SAM *(orgasm)* That's it.

≈ ≈ ≈

ANDY Thanks.

SAM Mmm.

ANDY That was great.

SAM Mmm.

They dress, slowly.

ANDY So.

SAM So.

ANDY When will I…? When will we…?

SAM *(smiles)* Whenever we meet.

ANDY Thursday.

SAM Whenever we meet.

ANDY   Come on.

SAM   I can see you from up here. From my window. I can see you when you walk into the park. When you sit on the bench. When you wait.

ANDY   You like that don't you.

SAM   What.

ANDY   Watching me wait.

SAM   Something about meeting outside.

ANDY   Yes. But when.

SAM   *(teasing)* You *are* impatient, aren't you. We'll have to work on that.

ANDY   I need to know.

SAM   Whenever. Trust me.

ANDY   Thursday. Four o'clock.

Pause.

SAM   I can't.

ANDY   Why not.

SAM   I thought we agreed–

ANDY   But don't you think–?

SAM   No pasts, no futures. Nothing. Just this. This moment. Remember? It's better this way.

ANDY   Experience talking?

SAM   Does it matter?

Pause.

ANDY Don't you, don't you ever want to feel loved?

SAM *(laughs)* Oh God.

ANDY Well don't you?

SAM No.

ANDY Don't you ever want to feel someone fall asleep in your arms.

SAM No.

ANDY Watch the morning sun dance on their face.

SAM No.

ANDY Taste their tears, see them smile, listen to–

SAM No.

ANDY Why?

SAM Because.

ANDY Why?

SAM *Because!*

She finishes dressing, quickly.

I see it all day, I don't need it in my spare time.

Pause.

ANDY So.

SAM So.

ANDY Sex.

SAM Yes.

ANDY That's all.

SAM   Yes.

ANDY   That's it.

SAM   What else do you want?

ANDY   I don't know, I…

   Pause.

SAM   I'm not your way out.

ANDY   I'm not looking for that.

SAM   Then what are you looking for?

ANDY   A way in.

   Pause.

   A second chance.

SAM   You think you're the only one?

ANDY   I don't know. Am I?

SAM   It's time for you to go.

ANDY   Am I?

SAM   Go.

ANDY   Am I?

SAM   Please.

ANDY   *(a discovery)* I am. Aren't I.

   Pause.

   Aren't I?

   Pause.

I'm leaving my wife.

SAM ...Jesus.

ANDY Not for you, not because of this.

SAM Why then.

ANDY Because.

SAM Why! Why are–?

ANDY It's time. It's not right anymore.

SAM For you.

ANDY For both of us. It'll be a relief. Believe me.

Pause.

Meet me Thursday.

SAM *(tempted)* I can't, I....

ANDY Meet me.

SAM You're asking me to...

ANDY I'm not asking anything. I'm not asking how old you are, or if you're married, or what you do during the day that makes you so sad. I'm not asking any of that. Just meet me. At the park. That's all.

Pause.

Will you do that?

Pause.

Will you?

He touches her cheek. She smiles.

≈ ≈ ≈

SAM Now what's interesting about what's happening here, is that it's completely normal. It may *seem* unnatural, but this tumour orgeonesis, this cascade of metastasis, this breakdown, is really the same process that allows almost all living things to grow: An apple; the heart; a breast....

≈ ≈ ≈

SAM Are you Darlene?

LYN *(distracted)* No. I'm, I'm Evelyn. And you're... Samantha, right?

SAM Sam's fine.

LYN Sam. So sorry I'm late, I just, uh, I just ran from–

SAM I thought they were sending over Darlene.

LYN Oh no. Didn't they tell you?

SAM Tell me...?

LYN Darlene's ill.

SAM Oh?

LYN A little accident.

SAM Oh no.

LYN Hot coffee.

SAM Ouch.

LYN First degree burn.

SAM God.

LYN One of those freak things. You know.

SAM Right.

LYN	So I'm taking her calls.
SAM	Right.
LYN	Help each other out. You'll find our office works like a team.
SAM	Right.
LYN	I'm so sorry I'm late, but–
SAM	That's alright.

Pause.

LYN	So.

LYN waltzes in.

You're selling.

SAM	Thinking about it.
LYN	Very nice.
SAM	Thanks.
LYN	New hardwood?
SAM	Yeah.
LYN	Paint?
SAM	In the summer.
LYN	One bedroom?
SAM	Two. The other one's…
LYN	Nice size, this bedroom.
SAM	Mm.
LYN	Oh my God!

SAM   What.

LYN   This view!

SAM   You like it?

LYN   Gorgeous.

SAM   Isn't it?

LYN   Look at that: the park.

SAM   Yeah.

LYN   The lake.

SAM   Yeah.

LYN   The trees.

SAM   Mmm.

LYN   Like a picture. So pretty this time of year.

SAM   Yes.

She stares.

LYN   Isn't that, isn't that, that bench?

SAM   What?

LYN   The one by the lake.

SAM   Ah. Yeah.

LYN   I know that bench.

SAM   Oh?

LYN   Don't live far from here myself.

SAM   Oh?

LYN   I've sat on that bench. My, my husband and I used to go there quite often. When we were first married. Looks so small from up here. So lonely, so....

   LYN stares out the window.

SAM   So. What do you think?

LYN   *(still staring)* Oh I love the park.

SAM   No. Of the place I mean.

LYN   Oh!

SAM   Think it'll sell?

LYN   Oh it'll sell alright. No doubt about that. It'll sell.

SAM   Great.

LYN   Now. I just need to ask you a few questions. Hope you don't mind.

SAM   I... suppose not.

LYN   Standard stuff. So I know.

SAM   Alright.

LYN   Why are you moving.

SAM   Well...

LYN   Problems?

SAM   You mean–?

LYN   With the condo. Any problems. You'll have to disclose it eventually, might as well tell me now.

SAM   Oh no, no. No problems.

LYN   Water?

SAM Fine.

LYN Heat?

SAM Fine.

LYN Foundation, pool, parkade–

SAM Everything's fine that I know of.

LYN *(smiles)* Nobody's after you?

SAM Pardon?

LYN Banks, creditors, collection agencies.

SAM No. No problems there.

LYN Working?

SAM I'm a, a student.

LYN *(suspicious)* Oh. In…?

SAM Medicine.

LYN *(pleased)* Ah! Good! If you'd have said Philosophy or English or something….

SAM Right.

LYN So how are you managing the place?

SAM …managing…?

LYN Well you *are* a student, how are you–

SAM It's my mother's.

LYN Oh?

SAM Yes.

LYN And she's, she's what, she's renting–?

SAM	She's dead.
	Pause.
	She…
	Pause.
	She died.
	Pause.
LYN	Oh.
SAM	Yeah.
	Pause.
LYN	I'm, I'm sorry, I–
SAM	That's alright.
LYN	I didn't mean–
SAM	She left me the place…
LYN	Of course…
SAM	…but I'm not really sure I want to, you know, live here…
LYN	Of course.
SAM	…so I'm just checking to see what it's worth.
LYN	Of course, of course. I'm sorry, I just thought: "she's a *student*…"
SAM	Right.
LYN	"…and what's a *student* doing owning…"
SAM	Right.

LYN	"…And it doesn't look like anybody else really lives here, no boyfriend, no *husband*, no…"
SAM	Husband? *(laughs)*
LYN	*(laughs)* No?
SAM	Oh God no.
LYN	Me. It's been sixteen years.
SAM	Really?
LYN	Sixteen years.
SAM	Wow. I can't imagine.
LYN	Neither can I. Sometimes.
SAM	He in real estate as well?
LYN	Oh no. He, well, he *was* in government, but he's… he's been laid off.
SAM	Oh.
LYN	Twenty minutes to clear off his desk. Twenty minutes for ten years. Ten years.
SAM	Oh.

Pause.

(a discovery) Oh.

LYN	Sometimes I—and maybe you'll feel this one day—sometimes I look at him and I… I don't remember, I don't remember who he is, or…
SAM	Things change.
LYN	They do. But it happens so… you hardly notice, you don't see things coming, and then it happens, out of the blue, something you never expected, never thought

about, never even considered... something pops, something twigs, and you... you....

She feels ill.

Do you, do you mind if I...

She sits on the edge of the bed.

SAM   Are you alright?

LYN   It's nothing.

SAM   Are you sure?

LYN   No no, I'm fine, really.

SAM   I'll get you some water.

She goes.

LYN   I've just been a little... I'm just a little stressed.

SAM   *(off)* Right.

LYN   With my husband not working and... and our marriage, it's, it's not....

SAM   *(off)* Right.

LYN   *(to self)* And now I have to, I have to....

LYN weeps. SAM enters. Unsure, she hands LYN a Kleenex.

SAM   Here.

LYN   Thanks.

LYN blows. SAM hands her the water.

SAM   Take a sip.

LYN   Thank you. I didn't mean....

Sips.

I'm not usually….

Sips.

I'm so embarrassed.

SAM   Don't be. You should see someone. A doctor.

LYN   Yes, well, funny that. I just came.

SAM   What.

LYN   From the doctor.

SAM   Oh?

LYN   Yes.

Pause.

Anyway….

She puts on her best face.

You're selling.

SAM   Thinking about it.

LYN   Well, I have one rule.

SAM   Alright.

LYN   If you go with me, you don't go with anyone else. We're in this together. A kind of marriage. If you agree to that, I'll be there for you. I'll work hard for you. I'll do anything to get you the best price for this place. If you don't, I won't. Plain and simple. Alright?

Pause.

Okay?

> *She holds out her hand.*

Agreed?

≈ ≈ ≈

> *LYN sitting in the park. ANDY enters. He sees LYN. He is about to leave.*

LYN   Hi.

> *Pause.*

ANDY   *(anxious)* Hey.

LYN   What are you…? You're here.

ANDY   Yeah.

> *ANDY looks around.*

Christ what a day.

LYN   Oh?

ANDY   Goddamn interviews.

LYN   Ah.

ANDY   Same old, same old.

LYN   Yeah?

ANDY   Too old for new stuff. Too young to be a CEO.

LYN   Right.

> *ANDY looks around.*

ANDY   I… I was looking for you this morning.

LYN   Oh?

ANDY   Thought we could talk. I dropped by the office, but they said you went home.

LYN   Yeah.

ANDY   So I went home. But you weren't there.

LYN   No.

ANDY   And so I... I thought I'd come here. To the park. Clear my, clear my mind, you know?

He looks around.

LYN   I wanted to talk to you too.

ANDY   Yeah?

LYN   I phoned home, but you weren't there.

ANDY   The interview.

LYN   And so I came home, but you weren't back. And so I thought I'd come here.

ANDY   Right.

LYN   Clear my mind, clear my thoughts. Like you.

Pause.

ANDY   Well.

Pause.

We, uh, we better get home.

LYN   I thought we were going to talk.

ANDY   Right. So we should get home. So we can–

LYN   Sit for a while.

ANDY   Don't you think it'd be better if we–?

LYN   Sit.

> *Pause.*

Please.

> *He sits, reluctantly.*

You remember...? Remember when you proposed?

ANDY   Proposed? Uh, sure, we....

LYN   Up in the mountains. A day like today. We made love on that cliff. Sat naked overlooking the lake. The smell of the wind, the pines all around, cut off from the world, our own little paradise. Remember?

ANDY   Sure.

LYN   And you said: "I promise to take care of you Lyn. Forever."

ANDY   Lyn....

LYN   "I promise."

> *Pause.*

I haven't been very nice to you lately. I know that.

> *Pause.*

I haven't fulfilled my end of the bargain, I see that now.

> *Pause.*

I haven't been much of a wife, or a friend, or even a roommate for that matter.

> *Pause.*

I'm sorry.

ANDY   Lyn, we've tried. We've tried. But we both know—

LYN I have a job for you.

    Pause.

ANDY You have a job for me. *You* do.

LYN Yes.

    Pause.

I went to the doctor.

ANDY Oh?

LYN I've been feeling tired and...

ANDY Are you...?

LYN I...

ANDY You're not – are you pregnant?

LYN No. No....

ANDY *(relieved)* No, no of course...

LYN No. I've got a....

    Pause.

In my breast.

    Pause.

I'm going to need your help.

    Pause.

That's your job. I need you to take care of me.

    SAM enters, unseen to ANDY and LYN. She watches from a distance. As the lights fade, ANDY steps forward, overlooking the lake.

ANDY   I listen. But I hear nothing. Until she holds me. Hard. And only then does my imagination shudder, and the tears spill from her eyes, down my neck, to my breast, to my own...

LYN   That's your job.

ANDY   She says.

LYN   To take care of me.

l to r:
Coralie Cairns,
Shaun Johnston,
Daniela Vlaskalic.
Photographer: Russ Hewitt

ACT TWO

> *ANDY overlooking the lake. SAM watches him. LYN in a different world, paring things down.**

ANDY   I stare at the lake.

LYN   "Poison."

ANDY   She says. I listen to the trees.

LYN   "Temptation."

ANDY   She says. I smell the fall air.

LYN   (*smiles*) "Opportunity."

ANDY   (*fondly*) She says. I look into her eyes. Not hard. But gently. Scanning her thoughts, searching her mind, surveying her trust. Until her mouth shivers, and a smile slowly spills across her lips, her cheeks, her face, spreading to my own eyes, to my own–

LYN   "Knowing."

ANDY   She says.

LYN   "It's about knowing."

> ≈ ≈ ≈

SAM   Hello, I'm Samantha, Dr. Herbert asked me to look after your file while she's–

LYN   Yes. She told me.

SAM   Oh.

> *Pause.*

Oh my God, you're...

> **Please see Production Notes on page 2.*

LYN   Lyn.

SAM   Of course. I didn't–

LYN   Make the connection.

SAM   The condo.

LYN   Overlooking the park, right?

SAM   Yes. Yes of course. So, so I'm guessing…

LYN   I'm on leave.

SAM   Right. Right.

Pause.

I'm Dr. Herbert's assistant. I'm an intern. I'm studying Oncology.

LYN   Yes. Did you do it?

Pause.

SAM   Do it?

LYN   Sell the condo.

SAM   Oh. No. Not yet. I got caught up in, in other things.

LYN   Have you seen my husband?

Pause.

SAM   I'm, I'm sorry?

LYN   My husband.

Pause.

SAM   I don't think….

LYN   He's supposed to be here.

SAM Oh?

LYN Don't know where he is. He's usually on time.

SAM He's, he's coming here?

LYN He sits in on my appointments.

SAM I see.

LYN All the goddamn questions you people ask.

SAM If you....

LYN I can never remember–

SAM If you want...

LYN The same questions, over and over–

SAM We can always postpone–

LYN Name, address, phone, occupation, pregnancies, abortions, birth control, smoking, allergies, family history, no, no, yes, yes, no, my auntie Jean, Christ! Can't think straight anymore, can't – and that Dr. Herbert–

SAM Perhaps we should–

LYN I have to tell you, that woman is a goddamn bitch. I know one when I see one, and I'm telling you that Dr. Herbert is one. And I know she's your boss, your supervisor, whatever, but I'm telling you she's a bitch, and she knows she's a bitch, 'cause when I first came to see her, it was like, like....

Pause.

She's feeling around me like I'm some piece of.... Makes me go through all these tests, all these.... Here for blood, there for x-rays. Meanwhile I miss closing a deal, a good commission, been working on it for *months*, and here I am running halfway across the city, not knowing what I'm doing, not knowing what's going on, not knowing....

Pause.

And that afternoon, she calls me, she calls me, and she says, "looks like we'll have to do a biopsy after all," she says, like I get this done every day, "looks like we'll have to do a biopsy *after all*," like I'm getting my fucking teeth cleaned. So I get the biopsy and that's, well what can I say, *no fun*, and I get called into the office, and I sit here, right here, and she says, standing where you are, she says to me, with a straight face she says: "You've got metaplastic adenosquamous cancer, I recommend a mastectomy with Taxotere and if that doesn't work, well there's really not much of a treatment regimen *without* cure, never mind a treatment regimen *with* cure" and I ask you, I ask you: *What the fuck does THAT mean?*

She is exhausted, but presses on.

And so I say to her "Dr Herbert, does that mean I'm going to die? Is that what you're telling me? That I'm going to die?" And you know what she says to me? Know what she says?

Pause.

"Some people see this as a gift. Maybe you have to look at it as a gift."

Pause.

And I said to her, I said: "Now listen to me, you goddamn bitch. This is a disease. This is a curse. This is poison. And don't you dare tell me… don't you dare tell…

LYN weeps.

SAM   We can do this later. Alright Lyn? We can….

ANDY enters.

ANDY   Sorry I'm late, I–

    A long pause, as LYN weeps. Finally:

SAM   *(to ANDY)* I, I'm Samantha, I'm Dr. Herbert's–

ANDY   *(quietly)* Please leave.

    Pause.

SAM   I only–

ANDY   Leave.

SAM   I'm only–

ANDY   Leave.

    Pause.

    Please.

    SAM exits. ANDY goes to LYN.

LYN   ...I'm not...

ANDY   Shh.

LYN   ...I'm not feeling very...

ANDY   Shh. It's okay. We'll get you home. We'll get you home. Okay?

LYN   ...It's not a gift, it's not....

ANDY   Shhh.

    ≈ ≈ ≈

SAM   Here we can see cells growing in a relatively uncontrolled fashion, separating from one another to begin invasion. With time, the number of these cells will increase until they represent the majority. In this case here, the tumour resides in the breast of...

Pause.

A married female in her, her early to mid forties.

≈ ≈ ≈

ANDY (*dishevelled*) ...Hello....

SAM Well hello.

ANDY Beau... beautiful day.

SAM Yes.

ANDY The lake.

SAM Yes.

ANDY The trees.

SAM Yes.

ANDY The park.

SAM Mm.

Pause.

ANDY Time off work?

SAM Yeah. Uh, no, not really, I... taking a break.

Pause.

ANDY Do you mind if I...?

SAM No.

ANDY I hope I'm...

SAM No.

ANDY I wouldn't want, you know, if you're–

SAM   Please.

          He sits.

ANDY   *(sighs)* Oh boy oh boy oh boy oh boy oh boy.

          Pause.

SAM   I'm sorry.

ANDY   Eh?

SAM   About what happened. I didn't know. Believe me, I had no idea.

ANDY   Yeah, well…

          Pause.

SAM   Are you… have you been drinking?

ANDY   Yup.

SAM   Why.

ANDY   Why not.

          Pause.

SAM   Have you… are you working?

ANDY   No. Yes, what am I saying. Full time, as a matter of fact.

SAM   Doing?

ANDY   What do you think.

          SAM is silent.

          Been doing a lot of listening.

          Pause.

Listening to the leaves. Fall off the tree. In our yard. Quiet, so quiet, down to the ground, one by one. They let go. They just... let go. And I think, how hard can it be? How hard can it be to just....

Pause.

There's this one. Big old apple. Sweetest bite you ever tasted. Perfect. But this year.... They fell hard. Not like the leaves. They fell hard. Just lay fallow on the ground. Birds wouldn't even touch 'em. Bitter, so bitter....

Pause.

SAM   Every day, I look for you. Every day, I stare down from my window. To see if you've come. Every day.

Pause.

ANDY   I have to tell her.

SAM   What?

ANDY   I need to, before–

SAM   You can't do that. Not now.

ANDY   I want–

SAM   Listen.

ANDY   I–

SAM   Listen–

ANDY   *I have to do something!*

Pause.

Christ, how can I, how can I....

He weeps. She holds him.

SAM   Shhh.

> *Pause.*

Come with me.

> *Pause.*

I can make you feel better, I can...

> *She doesn't say it.*

Just for today.

> *She kisses him. He responds.*

≈ ≈ ≈

LYN   Andy...

Andy...

Andy....

ANDY   Oh...

LYN   Careful...

SAM   Yes....

ANDY   Oh God....

LYN   They're not...

SAM   Bite....

ANDY   Please....

LYN   *(quietly, in pain)* Andy....

SAM   Hard.

ANDY   What...?

SAM   Yes!

LYN   Help me!

ANDY What is it?

SAM   Yes!

LYN   Help me!

ANDY What is it?!

LYN   HELP ME!

SAM   (*orgasm*) Yes!

ANDY (*wakes*) NO!!

ANDY breathing hard.

SAM   What is it?

Pause.

What. What is it?

Pause.

What?

≈ ≈ ≈

LYN   Hi.

ANDY Hey.

LYN   You're home.

ANDY Yeah.

LYN   Christ what a day.

ANDY Oh?

LYN   That old Chemo.

ANDY   Ah.

LYN   Flowers.

ANDY   Nice huh?

LYN   From who?

ANDY   Guess.

LYN   You.

ANDY   No.

LYN   Good. I hate these fucking things. It's like….

ANDY   Lyn…

LYN   It's like I'm already, like I'm already….

ANDY   They just want you to get better.

LYN   Yeah right.

ANDY   They don't know how to act, they don't know….

LYN   Yeah, yeah. Who are they from then?

ANDY   Guess.

LYN   I don't know.

ANDY   Guess.

LYN   ANDY!

ANDY   (*smiling*) Guess.

    She thinks. Then:

LYN   Fuck off.

ANDY Yup.

LYN No.

ANDY Oh yes.

LYN Darlene?

ANDY Bingo.

LYN Fuck off.

ANDY Bingo!

LYN Goddamn bitch. She's just feeling guilty.

ANDY Lyn.

LYN I'm serious. I mean how can she NOT feel guilty. The coffee....

ANDY Honey.

LYN ...the clients she stole from me.

ANDY *(laughs) Stole* from you!

LYN Goddamn bitch!

ANDY At least she bothered. You know how many people have called me since I left work?

LYN None?

ANDY Exactly. It's like I've died or something, like I've–

Pause.

(horrified) Oh God. I'm sorry.

But LYN laughs, in spite of herself.

I'm so sorry.

She laughs even louder and he joins in, embarrassed.

So.

LYN   Here we are.

ANDY   Pogey-man and Chemo-sabi. Another fun-filled Saturday night.

LYN   Clean the house?

ANDY   Yes.

LYN   Water the plants?

ANDY   Yes.

LYN   Take out the garbage?

ANDY   As a matter of fact I did.

LYN   Fuck you! Leaving me with nothing to complain about.

ANDY   Should I make a mess?

LYN   Yes.

ANDY   Fuck it up?

LYN   Yes.

ANDY   Give you something to be pissed off at?

LYN   Yes.

ANDY   Well then. I will: I saw a job listing.

LYN   Oh?

ANDY   Thought I might apply.

LYN   Really.

ANDY   Yup.

LYN   What a concept.

ANDY   Best to keep you on your toes.

LYN   What's it for.

ANDY   Really want to know?

LYN   Andy.

ANDY   You're sure now.

LYN   Tell me.

ANDY   Cause it may be hard, it may be difficult–

LYN   *(laughs)* I'll *kill* you, I will.

ANDY   Alright, alright. Ready?

> *Pause.*
>
> "Health Watch."

LYN   Oh for Christ....

ANDY   They need a book keeper.

LYN   Andy.

ANDY   What.

LYN   "Health Watch?"

ANDY   What.

LYN   A social agency?

ANDY   And what's wrong with–?

LYN   That's worse than government for God's sake. That's worse than *retail*.

ANDY (smiles) Gotta start somewhere.

LYN "Health Watch!" Christ.

ANDY Besides, it's a good cause.

LYN Ha!

ANDY Besides, we need the money.

LYN Do we?

ANDY Yeah.

> *Pause.*

LYN Do we?

> *Pause.*

ANDY Yeah. Yeah, we do.

> *Pause.*

LYN Fuck. I'm sorry.

ANDY Don't be–

LYN This is my fault.

ANDY Lyn, this is not your–

LYN It is.

ANDY Lyn–

LYN FUCK THIS SHIT. FUCK IT.

> *Pause.*

(*fierce*) Why is this happening. Tell me. What did I do that was so wrong. I never hurt anybody. Okay, so I threw coffee on Darlene, so I'm not a fucking SAINT, okay? But for Christ sake, is that any reason to do this? Is it?

ANDY   This has nothing to do with–

LYN   Look at me.

ANDY   Don't.

LYN   I used to be beautiful.

ANDY   You still are, don't–

LYN   Fucking liar. Look at me.

ANDY   Don't *distance* yourself from–

LYN   LOOK AT ME!

> *Pause.*

I have no hair. My skin is the colour of... nothing. My blood is full of poison. And you dare tell me I'm beautiful. You dare look me straight in the goddamn face and tell me that I'm beautiful.

ANDY   Yes.

> *Pause.*

Yes I do.

> *Pause.*

Yes.

LYN   I never loved you.

ANDY   Don't be mean.

LYN   I never loved you.

ANDY   If you think this will make things easier–

LYN   I. Never. Loved. You.

ANDY   What about now?

LYN What *about* now.

ANDY Do you love me *now*?

    Pause.

LYN Yes.

ANDY Well that's a relief.

LYN But I didn't before.

ANDY That's okay.

LYN *(sulking)* Only now because you're being nice to me.

ANDY I don't care about before. As long as you love me now.

    Pause.

    Well. I should go pick up some groceries.

LYN I'll come with you.

ANDY You certainly will not.

LYN Samantha told me—

ANDY You need to rest.

LYN I need to follow a normal routine.

ANDY Hey hey, I'm Mr. Caregiver, remember?

LYN Samantha told me—

ANDY *I don't care!*

    Pause.

LYN What's with you.

ANDY Nothing.

LYN   She's my–

ANDY I just think...

    Pause.

LYN   What?

ANDY We don't have to listen to everything she says.

    Pause.

    That's all.

    ≈ ≈ ≈

SAM   Hi.

LYN   Hi.

SAM   Hello.

ANDY Hello.

    Pause.

SAM   Well. I'm sorry to say this, but we're going to have to run more tests. We thought everything was in order, but....

ANDY What.

SAM   There's some evidence the cells have metastasized–

ANDY What?

SAM   The cancer cells, they metastasize, they–

ANDY What are you talking about?

LYN   Andy.

SAM   If you'd let me finish, I'd–

ANDY No.

LYN Andy.

ANDY I want to know what's going on in a language I understand.

SAM The cells grow quickly, they divide, they grow, they invade, and the whole thing repeats itself. We want to make sure there aren't any cancerous cells left. That's all.

Pause.

LYN When do I...?

SAM This afternoon.

LYN Do I need to stay?

SAM No, no. You can go home right after.

Pause.

If you have any other questions, please–

ANDY No questions. We'll be back after–

LYN What about sex.

Pause.

SAM I beg your...?

LYN Can my husband and I have sex.

ANDY Lyn, I don't think....

LYN I've been meaning to ask this for a while. Up until now we haven't, we just assumed, you know, that we shouldn't.

ANDY Honey, is this really the...

SAM   Some women report that after surgery, when things have healed, their sex life returns to normal and in some cases, improves.

LYN   Really.

SAM   Yes.

LYN   Andy, did you hear that, some women report–

ANDY I think it's time–

SAM   *(to LYN)* If you want to talk about–

ANDY She doesn't need to–

SAM   I wasn't talking to you, I was–

ANDY I think I know–

SAM   This isn't about *you*. Alright?

Pause.

LYN   Andy, why don't you go get the car.

Pause.

ANDY Lyn–

LYN   There's a few more things I'd like to discuss.

ANDY I was hoping that–

LYN   Andy. Get the car.

Pause. He leaves.

LYN   I'm sorry.

SAM   That's alright.

LYN   He's been under a lot of stress.

l to r: Coralie Cairns, Daniela Vlaskalic.
Photographer: Russ Hewitt

SAM   I understand.

LYN   He lost his job and…

SAM   Yes, you mentioned.

LYN   And then I got sick.

SAM   Right.

LYN   And for a while there, I even thought…

Pause.

SAM   Thought what.

Pause.

LYN   For a while there I thought…

Pause.

He might be having an affair.

Pause.

SAM   Oh?

LYN   Yes.

Long pause. They stare at each other.

But it doesn't matter now.

SAM   Doesn't it?

LYN   No.

Pause.

I don't know.

Pause.

From what you said earlier, I take it it's spreading.

SAM   We don't know that, we have to–

LYN   Your educated guess. Please.

Pause.

SAM   I'm worried it's spread to your, to your lungs.

Pause.

LYN   I see. That's not good is it.

SAM   No.

Pause.

LYN   Don't tell my husband.

SAM   Tell him what.

LYN   Anything.

SAM   Lyn, I...

LYN   If I want to tell him, I will.

SAM   I...

LYN   It doesn't matter. Alright?

Pause.

Okay?

She holds out her hand.

Agreed?

≈ ≈ ≈

ANDY   Oh God....

SAM   These cells...

LYN   Oh yeah...

SAM   ...these "forces..."

ANDY   Jesus.

SAM   ...keep growing...

LYN   Yes.... Yes...

SAM   ...separating from one another...

LYN   That's it...

SAM   ...invading... growing... separating....

LYN   That's it...

SAM   ...invading... growing... until...

LYN   *(orgasm)* Yes...

Pause.

SAM   ...things break down. They... break down.

Pause.

ANDY   Wow.

LYN   That was....

ANDY   When was the last time...?

LYN   Too long.

ANDY   Too fucking long.

SAM   ...In this case, the metastasized cells have spread to the lungs and also to the brain.

≈ ≈ ≈

ANDY   *(fierce)* Why didn't you tell me!

SAM   Because.

ANDY   Why!

SAM   She's my patient. Not you.

ANDY   You should have told me first. I should have been the one to tell her.

SAM   She didn't want that.

ANDY   You should have told us together.

SAM   I did what I thought was right.

> *Pause.*

ANDY   I can't...

> *Pause.*

SAM   What.

ANDY   I can't do this anymore.

SAM   Listen.

ANDY   Not now. Not now, I can't.

SAM   I know it's hard, I know, but...

ANDY   I can't, I can't, I can't.

> *Pause.*

SAM   Alright.

> *Pause.*

       I understand.

ANDY   Do you?

SAM If you can't, if it's not right, then I guess....

Pause.

ANDY Alright.

Pause.

Alright.

Pause.

Well then.

Starts to leave.

SAM Andy.

He stops. Turns to her.

When will we...?

Pause.

Couldn't we just...?

Pause.

I need to know if....

Pause.

ANDY Look–

SAM I need to know if–

ANDY I thought we agreed–

SAM I–

ANDY *What!*

Pause.

SAM I love you.

> *Pause.*

ANDY Wha...? Why didn't you–!?

SAM Because. Because I...

> *Pause.*

> I've never been... I never felt... I've never said it. Not really. Not even to my–

ANDY I *asked* you, I *wanted* you–

SAM I know–

ANDY And now, *now* you–

SAM I know, you think I don't fucking–?!

ANDY It's too late, it's, it's–.

SAM *Don't you dare, don't you DARE tell me it's too late, don't you–!*

> *Pause.*

> I know when its too late. *I know.*

> *Pause.*

> People die, Andy, you know that? People close to you, they die. And after it's over, you think "I never said it." I never said the words, I never told her I...

> *Pause.*

> But then it's too late, it's...

> *Pause.*

> And all you're left with is this hole, this.... And I worry. Worry it'll never get smaller. That it won't heal.

Pause.

So you stop saying it, because whenever you do, it's "too late" and before you know it, you, you forget, you know? You forget what it's like to say it, to say "I love you," forget what it means, forget....

Pause.

So I'm telling you now, Andy. I'm telling you I love you now so...

Pause.

So I don't forget.

Pause.

So I remember.

Pause.

You. That day. Sitting, staring at the lake. And I thought, looking at you, talking to you, kissing you, I thought, "maybe." Maybe here's someone who can, who...

Pause.

Who can heal me. Who could...

She weeps. He goes to her.

ANDY *(gently)* Shhh.

Pause.

SAM Do you love her Andy?

Pause.

Do you?

ANDY I, I'm sorry, I...

SAM   Do you?

       Pause.

ANDY   Yes. Yes I do.

SAM   Okay…

       Pause.

    Okay.

       ≈ ≈ ≈

ANDY   Beautiful day.

LYN   (*weakened*) Yes.

ANDY   Don't you think?

LYN   Yes.

ANDY   The trees. The lake. The air.

LYN   Mm.

       She coughs.

ANDY   When you get, when you get better, we'll, we'll come here more often. Once a week at least.

       Pause.

    Lyn? How come–

LYN   (*quietly*) Shh.

       Pause.

    Listen.

       Pause.

    Hear that?

ANDY Mm.

> *Pause.*

LYN Come here. Come sit beside me. Come.

> *He does.*

There's a few things we need to talk about.

ANDY ...alright...

LYN That I need to tell you.

ANDY We shouldn't stay out too–

LYN Shhh. Now listen. Listen to me. To what I'm saying.

> *Pause.*

LYN First. I want it to be simple.

ANDY What do you mean?

LYN You know what I mean.

ANDY I...

LYN You know what I mean.

ANDY I...

LYN You know.

> *Pause.*

ANDY I don't think we should talk about this.

LYN Andy.

ANDY It won't help.

LYN Andy.

ANDY	You have to save your energy.
LYN	We *have* to. We have to plan.
ANDY	I don't want to plan. Why do we have to plan? Who says we have to have a plan?
LYN	It'll make things easier. For later.
ANDY	To hell with later, to hell with the future, to hell with it. I care about this moment. This day. Right now.
LYN	And this is it. This is the moment. Where we talk about it.

>   *Pause.*
>
> I have to say this. Do you understand?
>
>   *Pause.*
>
> Do you understand Andy?
>
>   *He nods.*
>
> We need a will.

ANDY	…Jesus….
LYN	Listen. We need a will. We need one. I want you to call a lawyer. Get someone to come over this week. I'm giving you everything, but we need to make it official. Can you do that?

>   *ANDY nods.*
>
> Now: If – when – the time comes, you call my parents first. You call them first. Then yours. And you tell them to make the rest of the calls. Not you. Got that?
>
>   *ANDY nods.*
>
> Next. I want you – if you want to – I want you… I want you to feel free to, to marry again.

ANDY shakes his head.

I know it's hard right now, to think about that, but... you can't let this poison your future. If an opportunity comes around, if you get a second chance, don't be, don't be, I don't know.... Just don't be a fucking moron.

ANDY manages a smile. He looks at her.

ANDY And how am I supposed to know if the "right opportunity" comes around?

LYN If it's right, you'll know.

ANDY I don't think so.

LYN You will. It's all about knowing.

Pause.

ANDY You remember when I proposed? Remember?

LYN Up in the mountains.

ANDY A day like today. And the trees were, they were like a, a witness. Remember? And the air was, it was like a confirmation, it was so clean, so.... And we sat on the edge of that cliff, our legs dangling over the edge, staring down at that lake, like a, a crystal ball, squinting into our future. And I said, I said...

LYN "I promise to take care of you."

ANDY "Forever." I said "Forever."

Pause.

Lyn, I have to tell you something.

LYN Is this a regret?

ANDY I need to–

l to r:
Shaun Johnston, Coralie Cairns.
Photographer: Russ Hewitt

LYN Is it?

ANDY Kind of.

LYN 'Cause I hate fucking regrets.

Pause.

ANDY I'm rotten you see.

Pause.

To the core.

Pause.

I tried before, but then you got sick, and I didn't, I didn't–

LYN Andy.

Pause.

I know.

Pause.

ANDY I, I just wanted to say… I'm sorry.

LYN I know.

She puts his hand to her heart.

I don't care about "before." I care about now. Okay?

He nods.

One more thing.

ANDY What's that.

LYN I want to be cremated.

ANDY Oh for Christ…

LYN I'm serious.

ANDY Alright. Alright. Fine. Cremated. Fine. Whatever. And if I die before you, which I probably will–

LYN Andy.

ANDY –I want you to bury me. Put me down six feet under, so I know on judgment day, I can still crawl up from the muck, and prove to the fucking world I existed. Alright?

LYN Deal.

ANDY And what, pray tell, am I supposed to do with the ashes.

LYN Scatter them.

ANDY Where?

LYN On the lake.

ANDY In the mountains?

LYN No. Here. Right here.

ANDY On *this* lake?

LYN Yes.

ANDY Isn't that illegal?

LYN As if I *care*.

They laugh.

As if I fucking care.

≈ ≈ ≈

SAM The prognosis for this patient is poor. About ninety percent of these cases, these patients, these....

Pause.

The chances are, this… woman is going to die very soon. But. Prevention, early detection, new treatments. That's where we come in. That's why we're here.

≈ ≈ ≈

LYN barely conscious, her breathing laboured. ANDY, dozing.

LYN   (*very weak*) …cold….

ANDY   (*waking*) Wha…? Did you say…?

LYN   …cold….

ANDY   Well. We'll just have to warm you up then.

Places his body, or a blanket, around her.

How's that?

LYN   …mmm….

ANDY   Good.

Pause.

Lyn?

Pause.

I want to tell you….

LYN   …hm…

ANDY   I want to say..

Pause.

I love you.

Pause.

You know that?

Pause.

I love you more than anything.

LYN Shh…

He listens.

(dying) Shh……

ANDY She says. Until her mind shudders. And the last of her breath spills into my ear, down my neck, to my breast, to my own….

LYN Shhhh……

≈ ≈ ≈

The season changes. ANDY overlooking the lake. SAM watches him. She approaches.

SAM Hello.

Pause.

Beautiful day.

Pause.

The lake, the trees, the…

ANDY *(smiles)* Yes.

Pause.

SAM I'm sorry.

ANDY Yeah well. Been six months.

SAM Time passes slowly.

ANDY Yeah.

Pause.

SAM   Do you mind if I...? I hope I'm, I mean I don't–

ANDY Please.

She sits. They look out.

SAM   Every day. Every day you come. Stare out at the lake. Every day.

Pause.

I would have come earlier....

ANDY No.

SAM   But I didn't think....

ANDY No. That was right. What you did.

Pause.

SAM   Is there anything I can do?

ANDY ...no.

SAM   Sure?

ANDY Yeah.

SAM   You don't, you don't need anything?

ANDY A new job.

He smiles.

SAM   Is that all?

She slides her hand over to his.

ANDY I....

He gently takes her hand. Cups it in his own.

l to r:
Shaun Johnston,
Daniela Vlaskalic.
Photographer: Russ Hewitt

SAM   I understand.

ANDY   Do you?

> Pause.

SAM   Yes. I do. This is the moment, right? *(smiles)* When everything changes.

> Pause.

ANDY   Thank you.

> Pause.

SAM   I'll still watch you, you know. From my window.

ANDY   I'd like that.

> *She turns to leave.*

SAM   'Bye.

ANDY   'Bye Samantha.

> *She smiles and slowly walks away. ANDY stands, overlooking the lake. LYN in a different world.*

I stare out over the lake.

LYN   Goodbye.

ANDY   She says. I stare out over the lake. Not hard. But gently. Scanning her memory, searching her face, surveying her smile. Until my mind....

> *And the hint of a smile spills across his lips, his cheeks, spreading to his eyes.*

LYN   Goodbye.

ANDY   She says.

LYN   Goodbye.

Pause.

ANDY Goodbye.

He says, as the lights gently fade.

The end.

Photo: Nicholas Seiflow

Vern Thiessen is a playwright, dramaturge, actor, director and theatre educator. He has written for stage, radio and television. His stage plays have been seen across Canada, including *Blowfish* (produced at the National Arts Centre and Northern Light Theatre) *The Resurrection Of John Frum*, (National Arts Centre, Manitoba Theatre Projects, Landlocked Theatre) *Valentine* (Drilling Company, NYC) and *The Courier* (Theatre Centre, CKUA Radio). Both *Apple* and *Chaos* are winners of the Alberta Play Competition. *Einstein's Gift* won the Canadian National Jewish Playwriting Competition. He wrote the screenplay for the award-winning short film *Samurai Swing*. His play for young audiences, *Dawn Quixote*, was premiered by Quest Theatre in Calgary and has been produced at theatres across Canada. He has served as Playwright in Residence at Workshop West Theatre, the University of Alberta, and The Blue Heron Theatre in New York City. He is currently Artistic Associate at the Citadel Theatre in Edmonton, and President of Playwrights Union of Canada.